The poetry of *Boyish* exists in that sweet spot between subconscious and cosmos, where the mind can catch any inch of oppression and turn it into music. A genius, Brody Parrish Craig, operates a ghost rail line; gut-wrenching rendition of Stormy Monday driven in next to the steel. A book built with lightning, whispered in the soup-line, reading your fortune through scattered tossed bones and bayonet fragments. Watch the best friend you could not protect from a merciless onslaught of violent American hegemony, save their self and become one of the greats; proving that poetry is the cradle that society never mentions.

TONGO EISEN-MARTIN
author of *Heaven Is All Goodbyes*
and judge of the Omnidawn Poetry Chapbook Prize

All language is dialect— may it be as this collection is— of a queer joy and pain and grace and revival. sonically, structurally inbuilt with a muscled architecture, grown over with vines of place and god and sexuality—here is a poetics coming of age in itself, and in the world.

CODY-ROSE CLEVIDENCE
author of *Beast Feast*

Boyish is haunted by ghosts the speaker plays with, like "holy shit I saw him ghostin' in / my breath I saw him in the glass ceiling." Sometimes the speaker plays with what haunts them out of curiosity, sometimes out of frustration, sometimes out of love. In any case, it is through this play that they can "acknowledge the shape [they're] in," "The Choir Boy" & "Hymn" in them they haven't named. Reading the poems in this compact and powerful collection—never has looking back felt this much like moving on.

WENDY TREVINO
author of *Cruel Fiction*

BOYISH

BOYISH

poems

BRODY PARRISH CRAIG

OMNIDAWN
OAKLAND, CALIFORNIA
2021

Cover art by adam b. bohannon

Cover and interior design by adam b. bohannon

Typeset in Radiata and Trade Gothic

Library of Congress Cataloging-in-Publication Data

Names: Craig, Brody Parrish, 1991- author.
Title: Boyish / Brody Parrish Craig.
Description: Oakland, California : Omnidawn, 2021. | Summary: "Boyish
    engages what once thought impossible: a reconciliation of southern and
    queer identities, of upbringing, rebellion, and revival. The coming to
    Jesus moments of looking back, of liberation & reckoning. Each page
    exterior & interior revolutions. To carve space between. To cut-up the
    absence. To find oneself carried over graveled creekside into the first
    mouth's babble. As much subconscious as embodied desire, change holds
    within the white space and the formal play-language twisting the
    unspeakable alongside dense sonnets, a thicket of warmth & dissonance
    that holds a mirror up to puddled overpass & river. The landscapes of
    city's dystopia meeting the queer pastoral, where conservation often
    means what must burn down"-- Provided by publisher.
Identifiers: LCCN 2021002384 | ISBN 9781632430922 (paperback)
Subjects: LCGFT: Poetry.
Classification: LCC PS3603.R348 B69 2021 | DDC 811/.6--dc23
LC record available at https://lccn.loc.gov/2021002384

Published by Omnidawn Publishing, Oakland, California

www.omnidawn.com   (510) 237-5472

10 9 8 7 6 5 4 3 2 1

ISBN: 978-1-63243-092-2

CONTENTS

BOYISH

HOUSE OF RISING SONS

Younger when I met you. Dreamt you. Fed me Queen
Bees on the balcony. Cotillion came that morning
& my mouth stung sweet pretending I was a girl
Grown straight into southern corsage—you knew

I was their firstborn son
that wasn't ready to come
each Sunday
               we watched the weather
channel in your twin-sized as the hurricanes rose
with names of kids we knew conjuring danger

An angry fist the shape
I couldn't part with or without
Naming the rise in me & no

I never sucked the honey off but made a gilded mirror
from your portrait drawling in my throat unsung I of
Hurricane that sunshine cracked open & Cut
                                 Taffeta streak
                                 over the Gulf
                                 ridge blue—

Down South we called our father *yess'r*; mother *for
your father's sake, just do this once*—I never knew

That Blue Irreverent, Black-Eyed
Ho'Susanna, Kind'a Wild

       Until the Day I Watered at your Mouth.

BIBLE|VERS

Top to Bottom | scan my profile | For Christ's Sake | Sing Jesus'
Name | I gospel & apostle | Book of Vers | My rural bottom's
up | My crop/top | down along the road | a hym(n) in hymn | this
earth-bound angel | prophet/apocalyptic | horse | I ride | through
town | tonight thinking of men | I meant to be | To Be | a hand
that holds | a deal/another | made with bibles | a multitude | of
Fingers | marking place | between | them & their Vers— | this
vers | of red script brought | up by you | Bluff & Blush | the
metaphor for | Christ | this rock | I crawled out/under | To
Be | free—

HAIRCUT IN THE KITCHEN SINK

Couldn't feel when you nicked
behind my ear, but I know
the moment when you asked me

if it hurt. Some remake scarlet

letter on the tv. Classic as a book
unopened on the table, my hair fell
over the kitchen sink & for once
no man was hollering *rapunzel,*

screaming *let down, let—*

Down into the drain. laughing
Different then, I didn't flinch.

* * *

Down South, most bothered us
to make a living: we stashed ourselves

in crowded basements, mosquitos
pooled around our feet, we tucked

our xanax back in the church van.

* * *

In Louisiana, we learned warm baths
salve bites as children first, but then

we saw the trucks that came in bursts
of state-sent chemicals—we knew

we were the same then: you, me, &
the mosquitos. Not sure the moral's

the state uses drugs to kill off "undesirables"
or that the dampest rooms will always buzz

* * *

The Loudest if you listen. Listen. Listen—Let

* * *

Us swear upon the night
we buzzed our skulls
inside the dealer's kitchen.

How when the men
we stayed with slipped us,
Even then, we dreamed

of More—

CLOSET MUSIC

Who pulled the devil's music out my closet
    note by note by note. who held a hymnal
to my throat. a bible's blade I belted out
    a red verse & who hollered bloody lines

About satanic tracks. my friend who fell
    through church rafters rehearsing passion plays
"he could've been the Mary of his mom's dream"
    if not for toppling hell's new angel from above

& *So below* we played bikini kill
    madonna lit our halos. bathroom stalls
we lifted tongue & smoke. we held our hands
    together. *like a prayer.* inside the back pew,

We layed our hands. we splayed our songs. Aloud.
    & if I play these records backwards, now—
the record / held inside / my chest rewinds

    & Jarring / as a baptist's first / listen
to a misfits track / we splay / our songs
    & lay our hands / along each other's / lines
your forearm's Virgin / Mary tattoo: skull

    & Wrinkled / rose / habit / her skeletal
hands / bare & grasping / prayer into / her beads
    we kept that secret / for so long / rehearsed
passion / fell / from church rafters / into

A Different organ's / thrum / the bible's / pulse
red line / an angel's / passage / underlined
     our goddamned / beat / all loud / music to ears
raised hairs / our skin / uplifted / hell that raised

     Our Heaven's   /   Handsome / Devils   /
     Note by   Note

OVERPASS

Perched above the slide, Meg says the cardinal's her Nana coming
back. I'm nine or ten. I scoff *impossible,* I toss up *sacrilegious,* I promise
that's insane. Too young to know the symbols, the no-menclature
of some traffic signs, but I know this: the Baptists don't believe
in second coming unless it's Jesus. Her Nana's not Jesus & I sure
won't be a witch, though next summer the heat tried to burn us
both alive: I watched the barn swallows circle the porch fan when I
couldn't sleep, the barn swallows became my father as he left again
/ got "clean" in Georgia, & I watched too many musicals on the sky
blue carpeted floor. I prayed & prayed that even though I failed the
promise pledge at Camp Bluebird that summer, that even though
I lurched forward in the pew a little late, too late, the only one not
standing with the Lord of anti-fags & anti-sex in the pre-pubescent
congregation, I prayed that maybe then I'd be an Angel voted most
likely to be the anti-christ & they were wrong, I prayed if nothing
else I'd become a cardinal or a bluebird perching near the heaven I
can't get in anymore & now I'm tired, tired from the image of

a fag
gut
gutter
mouth
the built-in infrastructure of the spit or swallow spit,
   the hock one at the passing
car or swallow slur they sent
fag
gut
gutter
mouth

whose tongue leak no one needs to see those thighs whose passing
car swerves round us crying about strapless dress & we should pass
like whose-the-fuck-we-look-like, man made in thine image, whose
    face is pooling in the mud
under a concrete overpass
whose narcis' puddle trickles down into this city's intricately
    constructed drainage system
fag
gut
gutter
mouth
whose fist knocks at my bedroom window whose threatening to
    post my thigh high in the air
ass on the internet whose threatening to call the cops on the dildo in
    the living room
whose fist on the glass is a bluebird seeing a bluebird's reflection
whose trying hard to talk-smack-follow bluebird
mirrored feathers couldn't quite
shatter the barrier between
our mirrored
wings

diss course of speech and im- peached fuzz that's street side
catching minnow men who drank a 40oz of holy water up the block.
Party like its 1993. A toddler with a toddy.
Strut your stuff just like a hand grenade.
So New Orleans, I watch the sirens shotgun house the wedding.
A veiled threat of dawn vowing the moon roof shut.
At 25 I let Jesus take back the color wheel & hydro-
planed into the garden, into Dante's Kinsey scaled inferno,
two snake eyes on the slice & dice, we didn't start the fire
in the taped deck, in the wrapped fist, in the Tarot fortune tells
us let the radio play along & I
am born from the hick in hickory the switch & baited mirror
The surgeon asked me if the surge of skin was once hospitable
    (you laugh).
Welcome to the electric
sliding scale, the shock me therapy.
The dog got jumped by a live wire in the yard you mowed for years.
I yelped when someone told me it was over

EVERY GRRRL HAS A VISION OF HIR WARD-ROBE

He said my thighs were boyish,
big, said less to crush you with.
He claimed my body was a roadmap.
Complicated to read without clear-cut
direction, without consciousness, I turned
over like a cheek & found a cig-burn
on my back's blade. He said I was a hot one,
crush of filtered, photo, semen's spring.
Splayed across the front seat, cock blocked
view of the oncoming road. When he pulled
out & over on the shoulder, I skirted strangers'
questions. O ring cheap scar smoke eye gallop
tripping over six eyes, sex legs, crushed mouth,
nip slip, evidence, so many tongues, so many

* * *

* * *

* * *

Tongues. So many tongues to strip from shoes,
so many strings to take out bagged possessions.
Ward-Robe, white gown, white sheet, white page,
in the ward we ghost inhale & ghost exhale the thought
if only I was King here with my idle hands pulled on the shoulder
waiting for headlights to flick or brain-fire to be put out.

* * *

* * *

* * *

We put out & we live by promises of rings
& fingers in the right spot good job G strings
are prohibited inside the ward no strings
but men here laugh say fuck me baby as I beg
the nurse to leave me nightingales say here say have a
Quiet Room they cough up a cement cell they tell
me here come cry in do not threaten, call for help.

I call for help over & over on the land line ask for the extension
of the agents of the arm of god my *King says firecrotch. Says firearm.*
Says fired, fired, fired. I fire all the men with reclaimed wood & hobblehorse.
Then, some patriarchal god sweeps in & tells them No, I got your back.
If I turn back take back buy back tonight I won't weep won't

* * *

* * *

* * *

Weep))

                              My iris
                              is a waterbed
                              to poke a hole in

                              like a condom
                              would be broken
                              leak of fluid

                              am I really

just a boy turned over
like a mouth
a stone inside the park
that we flip over to find
some worms in there

the wormhole is
under my body's
stone brim
like a furnace

                    flip me over
                    & I speak
                    so many tongues

* * *

* * *

* * *

My hobby: dress I kill & later tell it sorry,
sorry, sorry, sorry this my neckline con-
fessional why don't you scoop out every
inch of fabric of my being / my lost sheep
little boy blue ball blue in the iris my ringed
pupil yes we clouded judgement vision this
here number you can call or even number you can be
perhaps statistic call tonight if you are lonely me myself

my hot line & my vein the roofie wafer body worm
hole wound-well-open Baptists dipped their hands
in me said O my idol-grrrl my idol how many licks
years does it / will it / take & does it take the edge off
take the edge off of a blotter / white the black-out
body out / to take communion tonight my bible curled
to ash a snake's tongue splitting at the seams I locked
the four men in the fire though I only know the names
of three. Despite, for every crime I see Abednego won't burn.

UNTRIMMED SONNET W EXCESS SUGAR

Alone, men can't get by on bread & biblical
allusion. Mary didn't know that God's
a fag. *So be it.* Dust to dust on backroads,
where gravel clouds the wheels, the windows caked

with manhood's image hum *"Home on the range—"*
of mountains churned beneath the tires lifted
as *thine eyes* in a forest chapel crumbs
of Gretel's longing in the stereo

"Where's home?" Her brother knows the witch I caked
mascara on my masculine their Lashes
or what I mean is Fairy, Jesus told
me, sang *now go—go tell it on the mountain*

or what I mean is Hansel licked each finger
kissed clean the corners of my mouth, *Go tell it.*

        Another verse we reckon'd no one'd sing—
        we'd leave unseen—& then we burnt the sugar
        or scalded milk, we locked somethin' inside
        the oven—If I scraped the black bits off

        my heart for presentation, *Lord forgive me for*
        not knowing what's too hot to taste to touch

HALLOW BE THY VEIN THAT RUNS

Lord, once I raced crawfish
across a parking lot, watched
pinchers pull along the gravel
as the teacher held her stopwatch.
We'd placed numbers on their backs,
but no, I don't recall who won.

Mostly, I remember the slosh
of river water in a pencil case,
the release of its tired body
into a distant lake. My father
laughing when I asked him
if they'd make it back home.
I let it out & cried, knowing
displacement. Wasn't long ago

I left the ward & jogged
the streets from memory,
landed on a church stoop
hollering: *if you're real,*
then show me, couldn't say
the word for *illness*, only
demon, teacher, Father, god
& God I wonder what
those teachers think of

seeing crawfish on the gravel now
if Jesus' tears were just as red
as father's word stood firm

inside the bible & if I heard
somebody open the back door
but had already turned my back

Would you resent more that I ran
or that they didn't chase me after?

Tonight I race the red script in me
to the red script that runs against heaven
& the river's father said God broke
the mold when he made that one:

Red current & rush, if a tributary runs
between my calve & clodded mouth,
then let it know what's run across
to skim the red of every open passage.

& hallow be thy vein that runs
across the city with its sneakers on.
Vessel. No, a tribute to Red River.

FEMMEDADDY'S PRAYER

God do you remember
when 45 meant vinyl?

I woke up with consumption with a berry in my mouth & Juice-
Fruit-Faggotry inside. no burial just vigilance. their baptismal all
    thirst. no slake.

All heavy metal. God.

Can you hold a candle
to my Wrist-Flicker?

Listen, I know heaven is no carnival. no golden ticket booth. but
    when my Altar-
Ego flicks & someone threats to light my cigarette. worse yet light
    right into me
sees my body as a film over the pond a scum or moving picture i get
    tired of explaining that

I am not in fact a drive-in.

the soundtrack to my stomach not a pit. all juice. my hundred
something pounds of flesh a cake i jump out like a lake each
    morning.

My Sugar-Lisp.
The icing on my breath

PASSOVER THE PORTRAIT

His blood or mine that's shed over the frame His blood
or mine that is our father's son & holy shit I saw him ghostin' in
My breath I saw him in the glass ceiling sissy Sistine chapel
Portrait yellow as a thumbnail as a holler as a welt & swelter
summer son of mother fucker what you talkin' bout appalling
I'm a palling bearing funeral a body burying your friends a
paper chain of bodies huddled black as swallowed throat the choke
of tears & choke of chain of family china cabinet broken open chest
of drawers of hearts & boxes boxers full of coin & toss & man
under bridge of overpass or cards emasculated garden
& listen son there are levels to this shit & How you hang
A picture with the tool & how you hang a picture by the stairs
& how their stares are hanging on the nose like crooked letters
Of a deadname crooked letter crooked letter You put somebody's
Eye out in Mississippi son strong as will & what's to be cut out of
Strong as jerk & moon & silver circle jerk & wish me well
Inside the dark water I baptized his nose in blood *what's broken
About you is what I'll never understand* because I dive
Bombed every family dinner like a barn swallow he fumed
with smoke I plumed or plucked a chord to sing a hymn & never felt
those joints should be rolled up in hotel bible paper son *Let's hope
the savior comes to get you out of this damned house* but who the fuck
are you to teach me right from wrongful shadow of a doubt—trajectory
of thought of tragedy of shhhh now stop & drop the sentence quick
because I don't believe in blood

SOUTHERN COMFORT

I know the difference between whiskey & the devoted
cousin who sings *if heaven ain't a lot like dixie* in his sleep

the nights I drove nowhere, body flying behind him, brain
unholstered after pounding shots in mamaw's kitchen & tonight

when the man strikes his thumb back toward the red flag
in the pickup bed, *gotta problem with that?* cocked inside his jaw

the red light grins red flag red flag a spitting image of my kin
I hear my uncle's promise clear again, *we'll lead the next secession,*

yes, the time has come to fight—At the dinner we don't attend,
my mother wards off relatives. Do they know the blood that's on

their kitchen window? Passover comes first, the come to Jesus
moments after. The red light grins red flag red flag, my head

hung low to pray in traffic, & I remember what they said:
hold your breath but don't you dare unfurl your fist. It's war in Arkansas.

Last night they called again at 3am, *the bouncer shoved me down the stairs*
for pissing like a man. It's worse to hear their distant laugh

because I'll never see their bruises, worse to know how quick
I'll click the phone. The red light grins red flag god knows &

if he tries to fight, I'll speak—the drawling of accent, or breath,
the southern bell I hide under the roof of my coffin-mouth (in cases

of early burial), same as the quick switch when the blue lights flash
in Oklahoma noon, the knee-jerk mouth reactions of *yess'r*

my foxhole playbook, the un-strategic kneel of tongue, the taste
-bud sprout of weeds, I think it's killer how I pull Loui

-siana out my mouth when stuck in a bind & killer how
I know it's privilege & some luck I make it out alive &

I think of when they got flagged down in Alma by a uniform
by another man whose mouth easily resembled all my father's cells—

how my boi's foxhole prayer was british & I barely heard them speak—
the breath—I think the voice box is a silencer or shot into the
      dark—not sure

how to say please let them make it out alive without saying please
      don't gun
the intersection— I think if I could hold them then,
      hold back the whole
way home, I'd say that fire only works on brim of stone,
      but I won't mean it.

The traffic only ends to meet his stare.

THE SHAPE I'M IN

Hidden in father's wardrobe suit & tied my tongue Mouthed off
to every man I drank under the tables Flipped the temple chairs & stools
I split my side A seam I spilt it all & laughed off blood U stained
my dress glossed over lip & hymn I glossarized the strains

of weeds in papaw's garden & on the dealer's scale one night
I mapped My stranded hair & clogged the sink drain with my shadow
I popped open another body like a beer tab like a pore I wept
through puberty & puberty as if I was a second coming

on a neighborhood watch list The Boy Next Door swears
on the bible I'm my own new B/F in the driveway,
Hungers for me like a meal I'm better missed *miss, can you*
please respond to my last question? Can you answer my last fifteen txts?

If I'd told U in a deeper voice about the voice inside my head
The Choir Boy in me who ran & crossed your red-filed nails,
Suburbia, If I told you the holes in my story weren't full
of taffeta or sacrifice but slaughter, gauze, I told U they were

not the ones you think of I want to name the Hymn
in me like water's shadow of the valley mine & Want & Take
& Want I want to take a moment to acknowledge the shape I'm in
& Take a lifetime to acknowledge the shape I'll make

THE SECOND SHAVE

I dropped the guard I used for my jaw's one liner & didn't bleed
or nick this time. But this isn't an ode to the sink-hole drain
that something shiny fell into. I know my face as larger than life
sentence, more than definition, my hot mess more than wit's split
end, my scent more than Father's aftershave. I returned here razor sharp.

This is an ode to the blade

that I oiled with thoughts of Magdalene at my feet. First born son,
anointed one, the stubble of a waking dream. My body was erected
in thine image. A monument of thick skull, polished nails, & cross-
sectioned divine. A king, a queen, a cross-bone flag. A skeleton
key inside your closet. My departure hinged upon return.

BABY YOU EVER SEEN A WRETCH LIKE ME?

I broke the fourth wall & the umpteenth mirror. Stained
the ceiling glass the steeple hot under my collar. White-trashed on
the up & up, I'm punch-drunk on confession:

At 6, I doubled over in the baptistry & won a goldfish at the carnival.
We both came sealed in airtight bags & terrified of floating belly up.

At 10, I pledged the promised ring & sang back Cash's ring of fire.
Papaw always put a cent or two into the offering & offering
At 12 I dropped the body's copper off the blade.

Once I coined the phrase *forgiveness* meaning what is cut will give.
Once I cut the lace off dresses & they cut the weed with lace.

Once I broke me off & sang *everybody knows*
what I am in for—Goddamnit, kingdom come.
A maze of grace. An altaered state. How bitter
sweet the sound I picked my poison bark
or bite or apple. Splitting hairs & story strands,
I'd say I loved the Prick but that would be to
save us from the dark plot you're digging in.
Thy kingdom come thy will be done If I am heaven send
me a letter with a sign with some calibrated calligraphy.

Send me not a bullet but a well.

I open the curtain; I close the curtain. I go to therapy; I go to the store. I fill the intake forms in purple gel pen to make it through the inventories. Awake, all night, I remember new pieces of information. I buy a rod to assist in opening & closing the curtain. I look outside the window.

* * *

* * *

* * *

Call me Angel. Call me Dust. I am a dime. A dime bag. Minnow. Something silver. Something silver. Sinking in the body. Of the river. Change. The men we carry in our hips. Who carry us down stream. Who carry us down stream and skim the skin. The skin. That night I was. That night I was a grl. Supposedly no angel. I treaded, tread, am treading rapids, rapid, dark; I am here again to ask you nicely: am I a wake, awake, a wake.

* * *

* * *

* * *

I have always been called 'sensitive.' I see a stage; I stand on it. I remember my mother pulling me from the staircase: "stop crying"; "you're making this up"; or "for attention". I find a curtain to open, to close. I bow. I clap. I stand near the curtain. Some body calls this art. Some body calls this grief. Some body calls this another meaning -ful or meaning -less performance.

Some body calls my phone and it rings and rings.

* * *

* * *

* * *

	snap out of it	snap fingers cracked blown piece
into the glass	snap out of it	laced weed & pop of PCP
into the glass	snap out of it	snap fingers cracked bowl cherry
		Babe

says any wing-man can *(flip)* on or for a dime I am a dime

bag or a minnow in the body in the river *(flip)* in quiet moments
when I see your kids' faces & *(flip)* inside the moment when you
handed over their picture menacing "I'll use a condom kiddo—" *(flip)*

* * *

* * *

* * *

I wonder if the cashier at Arby's has trauma too. I almost ask them
but instead thank them 3 consecutive times in the drive-thru, you
know, just in case. I hold my large ice water in both hands. *Think of
a cool glass of water, there are many grounding techniques—I suggest you
carry water with you when you write. when your body's had enough,* too
much, *take a sip and listen to your throat slake. taste the cool and trail
it through your spine.* I have spent five days and nights avoiding my
assignment. An impact statement. Not details, but how the incident
changed, continues to change, my life.

* * *

* * *

* * *

If I should die before I wake, *(flip)* me on my back like a good wing-man. Else err on the side of caution tape *I'm sorry* to the mirror. Play the fault line over yes *(flip)* over & again. I'll shave my head to skull to *(flip)* the tape the movie memory made bare. Bare back get back *(full-stop)* & *(flip)* over & again. To *(flip)* every image that comes back in speck of glass shoved in a hand a foot a foot-hold. *(flip)* the shattered self & fuzzy feeling. *(flip)* the scripture that skin reels away. The skin that reels away like film like story marquee trauma *(flip)* into the glass.

No longer on the cutting edge, shrink-wrapped I rarely come undone.

* * *
* * *
* * *

We'll start with the hardest, deepest rooted. if you're willing. then go from there. To hold truth like a curtain. A little flapping lid. My eye. my I. My I: another stage. Another stage; I'm going through.

* * *
* * *
* * *

When I walked into the white-vased room of the asylum. When my roses were at war & blooming bloodshot on the smallest dark green plastic bed. When the nurses called my halos areolas.

* * *
* * *
* * *

* * *

* * *

* * *

If I Should Die Before I Wake, please (flip) *me on my back.* I'm back. No
good wing-man ever made of angel dust & weed; I dust the record
off. To voice over our past, play god & ghost, to ghost, to write,
to ghost-write. A new version. To open the curtain. To close the
curtain. The flutter in the lid. I open the curtain; I close the curtain. I
go to therapy. I go to the store. Some body calls my phone.
I answer quickly when it rings.

FULL

there are hives of honey
hives of stress red crop
circles memory's sting
no bee keeper for those
warm summer mornings

after bodies spilled their blanks into mine
& the moon that cheap machine of light
I'd saved for a dark day
masked itself & slipped behind the comb of sunrise

*   *   *

my grandfather was a bee keeper
he wore thick gloves & masked his hands
he looked like a boxer in the early morning dark

in the hospital my grandfather eats cheese crackers
& his orange crumb covered mouth is a baby's again
my mother combs hair lightly with her fingers

*   *   *

in the psych hospital they fed us
baloney sandwiches on stale bread
we stuffed our mouths with leftover
reasons to be alive

parents grandparents our siblings
local honey in our kettled tea

* * *

someday I will wipe my father's chin
or ask if table manners matter to the dead
if heaven is the correct placement of a fork
on a table or a road

* * *

this day another graveled crook
thieving my body at the intersection
like when the apple tree was split
down the middle by some lightning
& my sister cried until we broke
the homemade pie open like a prayer

* * *

if I squint to know the moon is full
maybe I'll remember why I came here
I came here to get fed & cut the bullshit
I came here to cut the sugar on my baby teeth

NOTES

"House of Rising Sons" is an allusion to the folk tune, specifically
Huddie "Lead Belly" Ledbetter's recordings in the 1940's. He was
born in Mooringsport in the late 1800's, near Shreveport, LA
where many of these poems take place.

"Haircut in the Kitchen Sink" was written in response to
"Colosseum" by Jericho Brown.

"Closet Music" references the music of Madonna, Bikini Kill, & The
Misfits.

"Us Let The Radio Play Along & I" references the 'Kinsey Scale' (1948)
for sexual orientation.

"Southern Comfort" references "If Heaven Ain't A Lot Like Dixie" by
Hank Williams Jr.

ACKNOWLEDGEMENTS

Grateful acknowledgement to the editors & staff of the publications where these poems first appeared:

"Bible|Vers" + "Haircut in the Kitchen Sink" + "Overpass" in *Hobart*
"Us Let The Radio Play Along & I" in *TYPO Mag*
"Every Grrrl Has A Vision of Hir Ward-Robe" in *Crab Fat Magazine*
"The Shape I'm In" in *Gigantic Sequins*
"Full" in *New South Journal*

Appreciation to the folks in 2018's Open By Riot Laughter workshop & *Winter Tangerine* for holding space to find some of these poems. Deep thanks to all y'all at Omnidawn for the care, warmth, time & energy invested into this book.

Bottomless gratitude to Geffrey Davis, Matt Henriksen, Anh Đào Kolbe, Eszter Takacs, Noelia Cerna, Calypso Jane Selwyn, & Vicente Yepez. To tender horns & my angriest opossum—these poems wouldn't have been possible without you. And always, for the empty chair along/in the middle of the room.

ABOUT THE AUTHOR

Originally from Louisiana, Brody Parrish Craig is a poet & educator who currently lives in the Ozarks. They are the editor of *TWANG*, a regional creative project for TGNC folks in the South & Midwest. Brody Parrish Criag's poetry has appeared in *TYPO, EOAGH, Gigantic Sequins & Crab Fat Magazine*, amongst others. They can often be found by the creek.

boyish
Brody Parrish Craig

Cover art by adam b. bohannon

Cover typefaces: Trade Gothic, Malaga.
Interior typefaces: Radiata, Trade Gothic

Cover and interior design by adam b. bohannon

Printed in the United States
by Books International, Dulles, Virginia
On 55# Glatfelter B19 Antique
Acid Free Archival Quality Recycled Paper

Publication of this book was made possible in part by gifts from
Katherine & John Gravendyk in honor of Hillary Gravendyk,
Francesca Bell, Mary Mackey, and The New Place Fund

Omnidawn Publishing
Oakland, California
Staff and Volunteers, Spring 2021

Rusty Morrison & Ken Keegan, senior editors & co-publishers
Kayla Ellenbecker, production editor & poetry editor
Gillian Olivia Blythe Hamel, senior editor & book designer
Trisha Peck, senior editor & book designer
Rob Hendricks, Omniverse editor, marketing editor & post-pub editor
Cassandra Smith, poetry editor & book designer
Sharon Zetter, poetry editor & book designer
Liza Flum, poetry editor
Matthew Bowie, poetry editor
Anthony Cody, poetry editor
Jason Bayani, poetry editor
Juliana Paslay, fiction editor
Gail Aronson, fiction editor
Izabella Santana, fiction editor & marketing assistant
Laura Joakimson, marketing assistant specializing in Instagram & Facebook
Ashley Pattison-Scott, executive assistant & Omniverse writer
Ariana Nevarez, marketing assistant & Omniveres writer